My Spiritual Joy

My Spiritual Joy

EDITH
LAWRENCE,
M.D.

PALMETTO

P U B L I S H I N G

Charleston, SC

www.PalmettoPublishing.com

Hardcover ISBN: 979-8-8229-3109-1
Paperback ISBN: 979-8-8229-3110-7

" Keep your face always toward the sunshine, and your shadows will fall behind".

By Walt Whitman

Table of Contents

MY SPIRITUAL JOY

I wrote "My Spiritual Joy" to be inspired and to be enjoyed by others.

Imagine, I have decided to write these poems after my thoughts were overwhelmed with inspiration.

It started when I was impatiently waiting for a patient at a hospital emergency room.

I was sitting next to a fish bowl. For hours, I concentrated on the fish. Then I started thinking about how that fish had a story to tell. I, too, had several thoughts that related to tell about my personal experiences. I wrote the fish poem followed by others.

Children's endeavors and funny instances about The Cat or The Spider did not distract me from the Spiritual esteem of poems portrayed.

My purpose was to inspire others to know the importance of Life, through God's Will.

My personal history as a Christian was influenced by my family at a young age to present.

I am an African-American who lived mostly in New York City, until I attended The Sorbonne University of Paris Medical

School. I am a medical doctor and, the first Black American to graduate from this medical school. When I think that all my studies were in French, I wonder how it happened. (Perhaps in a new book I should tell the story).

The purpose of this book is to inspire a different format of poetry that would allow my feelings to be recognized. I believe everyone is inspired by God and He uses us, ordinary people, to do His work on earth.

I'm humbly grateful to share this book with you and hope it will inspire you to search for your purpose in life.

My plan for youth and adults would be to entertain a new awareness of Christian poetry that would enlighten their outlook going forward.

My poems will be a new introduction to personal inspirational hope for humanity.

Darkness

Don't turn off the lights, not just yet
My clearer vision must certainly be met

The night is young and anxiously seen
With joy of hope for tomorrow's dream

When eyes are opened for expected light
I understand myself with unseen sight

My eyesight is to hear and ears to see
True images of self that will set me free

Happiness is to be secured from God Above
With true vision of light and Eternal Love.

The Light that Shines

Imagine not having any light of vision
The darkness becomes a blindfold provision

How hopeful it would be for a thoughtful sight
That will realistically become instantly bright

How needlessly we regret for sorrowful pain
For not early expressing God's Laws in vain

Why not seek His plans for all humanity
In obedience to obliterate insanity

The vision to see shines in our eyes and ears
And propagate a manner in which we can hear

The voice of Jesus in Glorious delight
Will sound His Glory from Darkness to Light.

My Wisdom Eyes

How great it is that I can see
 God's Blessings that remain with me

My visit to the Holy Land with Biblical Sights
Opened my closed eyes in historical Light

The movement of spherical dimensions in slope
Delivered in depth the knowledge of Hope

My awareness of Jesus' presence stimulated my brain
With glaringly images magnificently vain

The blindness of darkness has not removed my Vision
From historical Biblical events in justified Provision

I am thankful for meaningful knowledge each day
That brings me one step towards His Pathway to Stay.

Reflection

Our inner thoughts work overtime shame
With past experiences of regrets and instant pain

Rejoice when over abundance will submit
A part of ourselves that cannot omit

As it creeps on us with anxiety restrain
A solitude's encouraging witness is pain

Happy are those who ignore sadness of thought
In reflecting past experiences, shared and fought

Be thankful for thoughts of laughter and beam
For encouraging beginning of momentum esteem

The greatest joy to be a child of God Above
Who will protect us with innocent reflection of Love.

Temptation

When I wake up from an awful dream
Is it okay to indiscriminately scream

I prefer acting out by withdrawing within
With unexpected thoughts of egregious sin

But wait a minute, I have strong control
As a child of God I was taught to be bold

Not to have fun in thoughts and deeds
But to pray to overcome temptation's needs

My fight is strong and I will certainly win
Because my Faith in God will overcome sin

We all are tempted during moments of fear
When our thoughts are deceived by our listening ear

Do not give up on accomplishing your goal
For God's strength and fortitude will make you Whole.

Anxiety

What makes a person frustrated and shame
Could I be responsible for conflict and blame

I'm not at fault that I patiently wait
For something to happen in an honest debate

No wonder my thoughts are in disparaging insults
I have been waiting and waiting for endless results

On elevated matters that affect upstream
My secret thoughts are mostly a dream

Don't talk to yourself and prove yourself right
When your answered questions are fancy bright

Think seriously about when normalcy was fine
And anxiety was not a problem in mind

I can cope with imaginary thoughts for fame
Because I enjoy fun not naming someone to blame.

A Positive Image

Why not imagine living in a beautiful mansion
With fine art and furniture exquisitely in fashion

My vision eyes would see sights to compare
The fairytale stories that were told in daycare

As an adult I still wonder how great it felt
Stepping inside an imaginary bundle of wealth

But to be fair to myself and always smart
I seek quality, not quantity to stimulate my heart

The images of thoughtful phenomena I see
Will substitute many negative sights in deep

My wishful focus will be admired in wonders
When positive images are shared with others.

The Mirror

When I look in the mirror, who do I see
An image of a person or is it not me

My thoughts can imagine what to expect
In seeing a form regardless of regret

I look closely for answers that I may share
The visibility of sight evenly clear

There is not anyone only a deep reflection
Imitating emotional feelings in introspection

I often wonder which part of me is withheld
For proof of my inner self in anxious rebel

My thoughts are embedded with true imagination
In deeper understanding and thankful admiration

For expression as a Child of God in mind
I will not see through a mirror in time

Truly God has given me Strength and Might
To abide in Obedience and follow His Light.

Our Family

When we engage our family to stick together
We don't speak about recent events or bad weather
Our welcome will deprive us of instant thought
With whom we love in conversational fought
What happened to a simple greeting, hello
That connects our hearing-aid excitingly aglow
We, as a family, should put thoughts aside
On differences and temperament that might collide
The stressful sights that induce self-defense
Can substitute hopelessness for common sense
When unrelated distractions dominate family's esteem
We substitute a behavior with cellphone beam
The personal insensitivity of weeping discern
Can ignore family unity with great concern
Let us compare the needs of helpless others
Like a family devoted to sisters and brothers
From baby to cradle and past advanced age
We love our family beyond accretive stage
Needless distraction will always be sincere
With our families we love in gratitude adhere.

Leftovers

Am I talking about the food I did not eat
Or perhaps mistakenly towards a downward beat
Which personality conquers your way of life
When behavior justifies an unacceptable strife
The experience of pain past due in shame
Fills ones ego with emotional blame
We begin our thoughts by being extra bright
By finding allegiance to ourselves in delight
The stressful deeds that haunt us true
Will be hidden in a distasteful point of view
Although food is meaningfully tasty in flavor
In past dilemmas with unimaginable waiver
The difficult admission is to accept our past
Of lingering thoughts of unsatisfactory blast
How great to accept mistakes as accessible
Toward a new beginning of loving the edible
Our positive thoughts will climb mountains of success
When our obedience to God becomes a Peaceful Rest

Character and Desperation

Is there a perception that I should know
On how to breathe in disparaging flow
My pride and instant refuge tells my story
Which begins in reflection of forgiving glory
My upbringing will always tell the truth
Of parental influence of characteristic youth
I am to follow their influence in thought
In every day experiences with wisdom fought
When I get anxious in thinking ahead
My actions become intolerably secretive instead
Character and desperation are a bundle of hope
With God on my side in definitive scope
He gives me a choice to weep in pain
Without hopeless thoughts expressed in vain
How grateful am I to climb the ladder
Of unexpected joy in laughter and gladder
My faith in God will give me Strength
By overcoming negative thoughts in magnitude length.

A Smile

When you smile at someone, how far can it go
Is it from cheek to cheek as it starts to glow
If you give a smile, I'll give you two
How many will it take depends on you
Imagine every person who looks your way
Your smile will travel far in distant display
It brings glory to your friendly eyes of passion
With momentous time of instant attraction
Your smile is more than money can buy
To those who need love would surely try
To succeed in a trustful innocent care
Start from the beginning, a smile then share
It can spread contagiously in directions unknown
To creative esteem from ageless throne
An entrance of joy without boundless despair
Will become a smile of happiness from God to Share.

Joyful Love of A Child

How easy it is to spread your Love
From one to another from our Lord Above

The little ones naturally give us delight
In watching their innocent faces in sight

Their feelings of shared love will fill the room
When unexpected dancing attracts us soon

The precious moments of children's expression
Will blend well to our happy impression

Who will not allow a child to dance in fun
Winning their independence had just begun

Bravo, little ones for encouraging our hope
And bring us closer to God's gracious scope

When we have innocent thoughts like a child
We will share God's Glory in humility mild.

Lola

Lola, Lola what a beautiful name
The song of joy will come with fame

When one reflects her instant birth with Love
We always thank God for His protection Above

As she becomes more independently secured
Her talented gifts will be appreciatively adored

The beginning of Lola's life was a dream come true
Already built in future knowledge of her youth

We thank God for Lola's Love and Care
Giving laughter and smiles in moments to share

Her special communication in manner of speech
Will assure her future goals in God's Hand to Reach.

My Expected Toy

If there are toys everywhere in sight
Cover them up in a gingerbread delight
Mommy wants to put away my thoughts but how
Can I decide which one I will take for now
I always enjoyed playing with dolls as well
But there are toys at home but do not tell
My laughter is sadder because I cannot see
Other toys in stores that please me
Will mommy deprive me of my only choice
To select a toy with a very strong voice
I rather stay home and begin to cry
Before mommy decides which toy to buy
The daily burden of happiness will begin
When I thank mommy and daddy for a joyful win
I'm a little child for a short period of time
There are many years before my age of prime
I will pray that Santa Claus will come to my house
With the dream I wish without any doubt
A good solution will become my best all
When my teddybear is waiting and standing tall.

Happiness

It's only because I'm a little girl
That I have fun in a delightful smiling whirl
When I wake up with the sight of silence
A dream of words are laughter and guidance
Each day when mommy and daddy prepare my food
Before taking me to my daycare school
I expect the joy of seeing my friends
Who make me happy again and again
Some are older or same age to play
But I prefer the ones who are unable to say
My toys are theirs which is not my decision
My leader instructs me to share in admission
I cannot choose one from another in time
It does not tell me which toy is mine
Should I share my toys with those who ask
In return for a moment of favorable task
A useful exchange is already built
With a better choice of friendship skill
Each day when I learn something old and new
From picture books of words many and few
I enjoy my environment with a sense of love
From the leveled ground up to the sky above
The beginning of childhood has become a joy
I cannot wait for the next phase to employ
Thank you mommy and daddy, too
For giving me this happiness and joy from you.

A Child's Toy

I have a new toy but what does it say
It looks in my eyes with a pleasant display

At the moment I squeeze his full big tummy
I know it is not an image toy nor a bunny

The joyful sound of music is heard
It gives me a clue that it is not a bird

With his friendly appearance and beaming eyes
I look at his face in big visual size

A moment of laughter will begin to appear
I know now it is my new teddy bear

My common goal of love is joy
To begin playtime with my lovely new toy

I know it belongs to me, I do, I do
His appearance is friendly and I am too

I thank mommy for this toy in demand
I will celebrate little brother with my first hand.

Emotional Vacation

What joy to spend a peaceful day
On a delightful vacation I must say

My preparation is near that I will enjoy
Moments of fun in deliberate employ

Imagine emotions at a hidden place
With family and friends protecting my face

The reality of fear is deeply within
My permission to hibernate myself within

After returning from a splendid time
I pray with thoughts of spiritual mind

God protects us in great Demand
For a peaceful fortress under His Command.

The Fish

If I were a fish what would I do
I would swim in deep water and wait for my food

If I were a fish would happiness be there
My success is to share and look far ahead

If I make a move to swim in my direction
I might not be tempted to find new reflection

It's not bad being a fish at all
Who gets the attention that may always fall

Give me water, give me food
Let me do what is best in mood

My freedom and gratitude is to be blessed
As a fish I do the most and not the less.

The Cat

Why did you invite me to your house
Was it to be spoiled or catch a mouse

I prefer my joyfully independent time
Not to be distracted with rodents in mind

I like myself to do as I please
My advise is to give them your delicious cheese

The solution will end without doubt and help
You will be independently reassured by yourself

The will to do nothing can be anxiously asked
Am I not a professional cat willfully masked

The moment of complaint keeps me awake
I forbid anyone to interrupt my take

Being a leisure cat is not bad at all
I please everyone and still have a ball.

The Spider

Where did the huge spider really go
Was it on the flat wall appearing to float

Did my eyes instantly deceive me and when
Could I not approach it and just then

I need a solution I know not well
My obligation is to remove it and then yell

The gaze of stillness misleading in between
The already sudden movement of swiftness seen

This spider is prepared to stay and fight
And remain alive with all its might

I know, I know but what can I say
I do not want the spider to go away

In truth, it has a right to live as well
As you and me, so do not tell.

Disappointment

When the air is flowing with disappointed fear
I change direction from far to near
The manner of hope will stem from behind
By looking in a gaze tendered in mind
We are weak but strong to accept our fate
In passing our thoughts through an opened gate
Are we alone in darkness of sorrow
Or do we have hope for joy of tomorrow
Our thoughts rise high for a fight to succeed
With Faith in God who planted His seed
We are protected from all battles of remorse
From recurring rescues of inner self-thought
Yes, disappointments are experiences that can be shared
With Almighty God who is planning ahead
A new direction will follow His Love
For happiness and joy that will come from Above
The gladness of success in a moment of time
Will no longer become a disappointment in mind.

The Innocent Children

The innocent children were helplessly slain
Our worthless thoughts are difficult to explain

Tragedy in society must begin to end
With "thoughts and prayers are with you" Amen

Those little children and teachers, too
Were not able to protect their innocent due

They were welcomed into our Lord's kingdom in Glory
For the time of anguish to unexpected flurry

Let us pray for children"s safety far ahead
And maintain our Faith from evil-doers dread

Keep Faith alive with Forceful Witness
To abide in obedience in measurable Fitness

Our Prayers will be heard and reverently expressed
With Love of our souls that are already Blessed

Thank you, Lord, for Spiritual Strength
For Forgiveness and Love that will never End.

The Pill

We take our daily pill to keep us well
By giving us strength but who can tell
The moment of thought can cure our hope
With expected joy in desirable scope
When we take a pill to maintain a life
Our health is encouraged in satisfactory delight
Could the unborn be allowed this joy as well
By accepting God's Promises in human excel
Only in self defense are we to bear
The opposing cries in constant fear
The unborn destiny has constantly changed
From research debris to medical domain
The honest purpose for taking a pill
Is to be well and continue our life at will
By ignoring our Creator who made you and me
Human life in our time is rejected not to be
Respect the life that continues after us
From generation to generation in God we Trust.

My Dream

What joy I have when I have a dream
Although facial expression does not scream
I like my conversation with Jesus in mind
He tells me what happens in moments of time
Imagine an infant who constantly converse
In a glorious conversation with Jesus immerse
With facial grins that reveals His Blessings
My dream becomes uplifted as a child refreshing
We praise our little ones for silent awareness
And give Honor and Glory to God in nearness
The start of life becomes a book of dreams
That gives an infant its innocent means
Thank you for parents who nurture your best
In protecting their growth towards unending rest
I will continue my silent conversation with God
Who will protect me from the evil one's odd
Lay hold on life and it will be
All joy and crown Eternally.

Procrastination

How much fun it is to waste time
I'd put off my real project to relax my mind

I have tomorrow, the next day and always forever
To put all my smart thoughts in a bundle together

I don't regret being lazy at all
I'm too busy having a splendid ball

Who knows, I might consider doing my thing
If it doesn't take too much of my leisure swing

Okay, I got it, I must concentrate on me
Even if I have to sacrifice my innocent spree

I guess it's okay to get some things done
But I will rethink my choice and continue my fun.

Challenges

Must I walk alone on a road of debris
Or do I have a choice to set thoughts free

It takes courage to change my direction in time
When I allow sorrowful regrets entertain my mind

No, I don't always go that way
My strength and courage will become my day

I can walk in a direction and see the sight
When expectation of thought becomes ready to fight

Yes, we all have encouraging challenges to combat
But with God, we enjoy His Spiritual Contact.

Exhausted

How overtired and unresponsive am I to be
When awakened from a very uncomfortable sleep
The slowly dreams of hope for tomorrow
Will not bring daylight joy without sorrow
The burden of routine work is defined
With overtime thoughts in protests sublimed
The innermost self is not working to see
When my busy schedule is focused just on me
An initiative image of prospective hope
Will remove my ideas demanded in scope
Yes, God has a better Plan to explore
With Faithful prayers to Him and more
His peaceful acceptance is truly a delight
When my fulfilling joy is exuberant in might
How great it is to have His love to share
With family and friends in uncertain fear
There will not be hardship nor uncomfortable feeling
With Faith in God forever Appealing.

Myself

Am I weeping for more clouds to come
Or am I experiencing the hot blazing sun

For matters that are often taught each day
Those notions that will haunt me in display

Without a solution for happiness will I dwell
A new beginning in asking God for help

The joy of life has brought gladness to me
With requests in prayers for hope to be

The beauty in nature reflects innocent thought
To the Divine image that cannot be fought

Days and years will slumber with fear
Of discouraging moments past in despair

Imagine how grateful life would be
When my faithful thoughts are duty free

I will give Faith, Love and Hope for self offense
By accepting Obedience to God in my Defense.

Regrets

Joy and sorrow are two in one
Which decision comes first before it's done

Each day our awareness is captured by thought
By choice of blind allowance of inner-self fought

Our aim should accomplish joy instead of sorrow
With yesterday's hope for a better tomorrow

It is easy to say but difficult to digest
The experience present in temporary unrest

The boundary that surrounds an imaginary light
Will reflect unexpected experiences of sorrowful fright

Hold off and don't succumb pathways of sorrow
Before the day of joy would reward your tomorrow

Thank God for your Spiritual Strength from Above
Forever be Blessed with His joyful Love.

The Vision of God

The vision shared by our Almighty Lord
Gives infinite sights reverently adored

His chosen image of humanity is allowed
With Jesus' resurrection already borrowed

When Jerusalem was chosen in Biblical sight
We captured His meaningful direction of Light

Our Trust and Faith have empowered His Love
With unspoken words only shared from Above

We will always be thankful for moments of Strength
By glorifying His sights in mortal event

Let us continue His expected image in time
And always thank God for His Vision Divine.

Creation

What happened to the world that was given to us
When God gave life to humans from dust
His spectacular creation greatly dispersed from Above
In a world of Hate instead of Love
We walk and talk anguishing in pain
From sinful temptation of Satan in vain
God sent His Son, Jesus to guide us through life
To fight our battles confronted day and night
He insigne His Grace on temporal earth
With blindfolded darkness in Creative worth
Our protection from material reign of aggression
Will accord direct avenues in selfish possession
We appreciate all Creation in Almighty God's Hand
And standup to allegiance in stedfast demand
From a disappointing habitat that is not clear
To an unjust behavior of mankind's sphere
The meaningful Love of God's Merciful Power
Will give appreciation and forgiveness today and tomorrow.

The Trees

My eyes are borrowed to see beauty in sight
With trees dispersed in assembly light
All leaves and branches are unequal in shape
That gives promises of God's perfect make
My mortal mind can never understand
The power of our Almighty Creator at hand
With a vast disperse of tree types unknown
We enjoy the beauty of earthly throne
He gives minute vision that can be seen
Through His Eternal Rewards from Him to me.
 When trees are destroyed by fire and weather
Our thoughts have sympathy and regrets forever
The way of The Lord is to create Supreme Hope
For accepting His warning with an innocent Poke
Our disobedience of not following His Command
Has affected the earth in no man's land
It is with fear that Evil has prevailed
Until Jesus returns to His promising trail
The greatest hope and love overdue
Will be our God to restore a birth Anew.

The Clouds

As a child looking up at the clouds in mind
What images of beauty becomes divine
The bright eyes innocently shining its beam
Will sense a glaringly image momentous dream
Although the distant sight may blurrily appear
From an unknown height that cannot bare
This beautiful formation dispensed in the sky
Gives God's creativity a magnificent ply
How grateful for clouds to produce our rain
And water His earth from hills to plain
Thank God for His Blessings that are well known
For our appreciation for His Grace forever shone
We look through our eyes in vision yet seen
The unexpected depth of image serene
A child's clear vision is often employed
With happiness and love that is always enjoyed.

The Earthquake

A peaceful sound of tumult distress
Spreads angrily towards destructive unrest

Do I have time to say a prayer
That safety is on it's way from fear

Am I witnessing an earthquake, yes
With buildings shaking at its very best

The first to feel a part of me
As scared and helpless in what I see

My faith in God is not in vain
He knows my anxiety of instant pain

I will not give up and nor will He
With Assurance and Love for Eternity.

The Moment of Thought

Our eyes are taught to listen and hear
What would we learn if we could not bare

The moment of time, the night as it falls
The truth of our Creator is Wisdom for all

How great is our love for those we adore
To allow His Holy Spirit within us more

By gathering in churches to worship with Love
Our prayers for forgiveness will reflect from Above

His Mansion is prepared forever to be
Abundantly Loved for Eternity.

My Bubble

Have you seen my Bubble today
Its visibility is not sure to stay

My joyful thought has disappeared in sight
Not knowingly when it will appear in might

The noise accompanied all manner of sound
Would need to escape the silence abound

The hidden Bubble is sure to feed
A refuge defense of innocent breed

My love of self will seldom arise
Since the Bubble's option is a bit surprise

Give Hope and restful joy, I say
To my Faith in God employed each day

Only my Savior will set me free
When He bursts the Bubble that imprisoned me.

My Faith

Where is my Faith when hard times appear
I can look into my inner spirit without any fear

Could it be found in a lack of courage
When thoughts of despair are filled with rummage

I believe my faith in God is everlasting seen
With Spiritual Strength focused on me

God guides me through a tunnel of Hope
With assurance and obedience in stedfast scope

My Faith is always grateful to be
His eternal fortress with Hope for me.

Who Am I

Who am I or must I say
Just a person who lives day by day

I am an ordinary person well said by friends
Who respect my decision with optical lens

I cannot resist obstacles that pass my way
Since it does not dictate duties each day

There's nothing extraordinary that money could buy
That would put me in jeopardy with instant pride

Why not be acceptable to perform God's Will
And be used by Him with ordinary skill

The devotion and obedience will certainly follow
 His Plan and Purpose for my tomorrow

Truly God uses us all for His Pleasure
And renders us Joy and Love Forever.

ACKNOWLEGEMENTS

My heartfelt thanks to my parents who taught me to love the Lord always. They fostered an emphasis on quality and not quantity in my present lifestyle.

I'm grateful for the learning experiences and influences from my brother and sisters. Also, for my husband who had patience and endurance in accepting my spiritual thoughts during our marriage.

Above all, I thank my 2 daughters for accepting my spiritual determination to go forward with this book.

Without the encouragement of all family members and friends, this book might have been only a dream.

Edith Lawrence, M.D.,

born in Manhattan and raised amidst the musical heritage of Harlem, overcame barriers as an African-American woman to study medicine in Paris. She was chairperson of the Board of Trustees at Edmonds Community College and also participated in special programs for the handicapped. Her extensive medical background includes contributions to groundbreaking DNA research. Besides her dedication to medicine, Edith is a passionate patron of the arts, enjoying music, travel, and culinary adventures. Residing in Edmonds, Washington, she draws inspiration from her family's legacy of perseverance, talent, and unwavering faith. My Spiritual Joy marks her debut in the literary world, illuminating her deep spiritual connection and love for God.